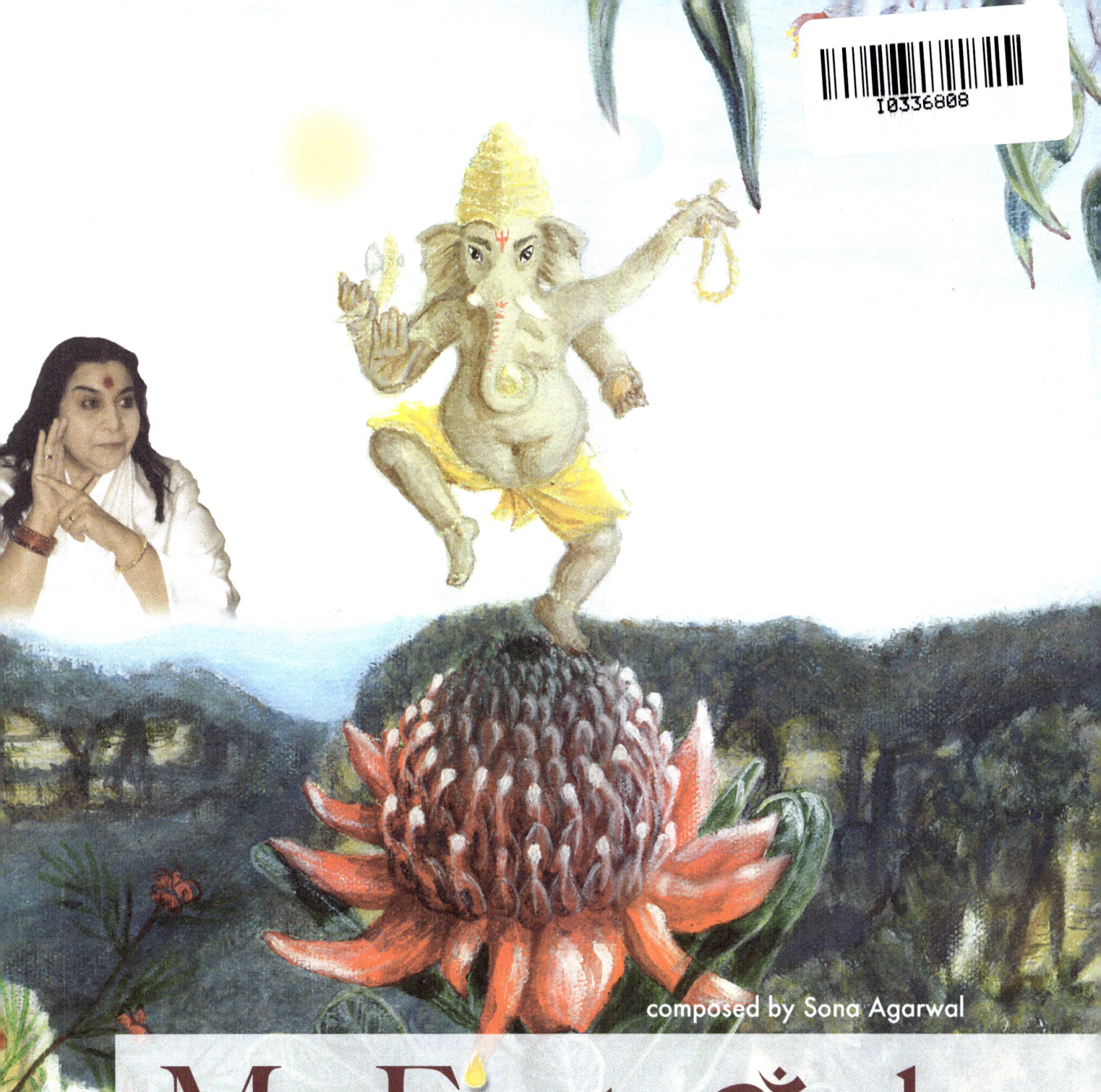

composed by Sona Agarwal

My First Book of Chakras

illustrated by Shanti Ghosh, Jeff Raum,
Jana Dallosova, Pragya Pradhan

Book compiled by Sona Agarwal
Painters:
Shanti Ghosh - book cover, pages 20, 31, 39, 40, 45, 47, 51, 59, 61, 71
Jeff Raum - pages 7, 11, 35, 43
Jana Dallosová - pages 3, 12, 17
Nejla Yaya Umapathy - page 38
Pragya Pradhan - pages 38, 55
Dasa Zlochova - page 23
Sunita Nath - page 52
Sona Agarwal - pages 25, 22, 27, 41, 62, 65
Aditi Heltberg - page 24
Ekaterina Denisova - page 26
Shri Devi Avilala - page 67

Special thanks to: Monika Shinde, Shamik Ghosh, Himani Naikare, Walter Lerchner, Aparna Lerchner, Radha Cody, Alia Einstein Diez, Flurina Wollenberger, Garima Singh, Trisha Pearce, Nitin Guje
Book designed by Sona Agarwal.

Second edition published 2015

(c) Vishwa Nirmala Dharma 2015
All rights reserved. No part of this publication may be reproduced, stored in a retrieval system or transmitted, in any form or by any means, electronic, mechanical, photocopying, recording or otherwise, without the prior permission of the copyright holder.

www.sahajabooksforchildren.com

Book dedicated to

Her Holiness Shri Mataji Nirmala Devi

... *"The knowledge part of Sahaja Yoga is very easy.
Anybody who is intelligent enough can read
about the chakras and give lectures.
But it is compassion and knowledge, hand in hand,
that make a Sahaja yogi...
The combination of these two actually emit vibrations."*

- *H.H. Shri Mataji Nirmala Devi*
The essence of self-respect, 27.5.1989

Contents

Mooladhara chakra (center)	6
Mooladhara chakra (right)	10
Kundalini	13
Swadisthana chakra	16
Nabhi chakra	22
Void	26
Heart chakra (center)	30
Heart chakra (left)	34
Heart chakra (right)	38
Vishuddhi chakra	42
Hamsa chakra	46
Agnya (center)	50
Agnya (right)	54
Sahasrara chakra	58
Ida nadi (left channel)	62
Pingala nadi (right channel)	66
Sushumna nadi (central channel)	70

MOOLADHARA CHAKRA

Deity:	Shri Ganesha
Number of petals:	4 Petals
Body parts:	Excretory organs
Flower:	Hibiscus
Musical instrument:	Shehnai
Color:	Coral red
Fruit:	Coconut, pomegranate
Element:	Earth
Country:	Australia
Vehicle:	Mouse
Location on hands:	Heel of palm
Precious stone:	Coral
Symbol:	Swastika
Planet:	Mars
Qualities:	Innocence, wisdom, chastity, purity
Cause of obstruction:	Impure attention
Clearing:	Sit on the Mother Earth as much as possible

TUESDAY

Shri Ganesha is very powerful, yet playful. He gets very angry with anyone who is against His mother, Shri Parvati. He is the one who informs the Kundalini when it is time to awaken, and it is His anger which produces the heat in the subtle system. He is the remover of all obstacles. The wisdom of Shri Ganesha is the wisdom of the heart.

Mooladhara is found at the root of the subtle system.

Ganesha Symbolism:

Shri Ganesha has a big head, because He thinks big. His small eyes show His focused attention. His long trunk stands for high efficiency and for His capacity to adapt to any situation. His large ears make for good listening, and His small mouth shows that He talks very little. His large stomach enables peaceful digestion of all that is good and bad in life. Shri Ganesha rides a little mouse, symbolizing His control over His desires, which, unless under control, can cause havoc. One should reign in one's desires and keep them under control. Shri Ganesha's one tusk shows us that He holds on only to good habits and gives up all that is bad and destructive.

What planet am I? (sraM)

Coral

Stone idols which have come spontaneously out of the Mother Earth are called swayambhus.

Shri Ganesha's Creation

Goddess Parvati decided that She wanted a son of Her very own. She used clay and oil from Her skin to sculpt a little boy. She brought the boy to life and named Him Ganesha. Shri Ganesha resides inside everyone's Mooladhara chakra. Just as He guarded goddess Parvati's bath house, He guards our Kundalini. He is the general of the army of ganas, or angels, that are constantly protecting realized souls and children. Shri Ganesha's army is the most powerful in the whole universe, and no one can stand in His way! That is why He is the `Remover of Obstacles'. If you have a problem, you can pray to Lord Ganesha and He will remove the problem for you.

Uluru Mountain, Australia

Shri Ganesha manifested in Australia as Uluru which is a very big mountain that looks like Shri Ganesha.

The **Mooladhara chakra** is made of the earth element and represents the beginning of life. When the Mooladhara awakens, the earth element manifests as a magnetic force within the person. For instance a person with a strong Mooladhara has a good inner sense of direction.

— Shri Mataji Nirmala Devi

One day goddess Parvati asked Her two sons to play a game - they were to race around the Mother Earth to see who would be the fastest. Shri Kartikeya jumped on His swift peacock with a laugh and started to fly! Little Shri Ganesha sat on His tiny mouse and cocked His head, thinking. I can't run as fast as my brother - but I don't have to. My Mother is right here, and She is the Mother Earth!" Shri Ganesha, representing the powers of innocence and wisdom, He sat on His mouse and circled around His mother, goddess Parvati. By the time His brother Kartikeya came back, little Shri Ganesha was happily sitting with the prize for winning the race - eating a big bowl of sweets!

How Shri Ganesha got his Elephant Head

Goddess Parvati decided that She wanted to take a bath. She told Her beloved son, Ganesha, to guard Her bath house and not let anyone enter until She was finished. With complete loyalty to His mother, Ganesha stood in front of the bath house's door. When Lord Shiva came to the door, little Ganesha would not let him pass. Lord Shiva did not know who this child was that dared to disobey Him. In a rage He cut off the child's head in order to pass into the house. Fortunately, the power of innocence cannot be killed.

When goddess Parvati learned what had happened, Her anger knew no bounds! Lord Shiva then realized that the little boy was the goddess's son. He knew He must make up for His mistake and He left the house and went into a field. The first creature that He saw was a baby elephant with one tusk. He beheaded the baby elephant and put the head on the body of little Shri Ganesha. The moment He did so, He came back to life - but now with the head of an elephant.

Stonhenge is another swayambhu of the Mother Earth, found in England. (These are the stones which emit vibrations.)

Questions and Answers:

Question	Answer
What is the Uluru?	- A swayambhu of Shri Ganesha
What element is the Mooladhara made of?	- The earth element
Who is the leader of the Ganas?	- Shri Ganesha
Who is the second incarnation of Shri Ganesha?	- Jesus Christ
Who is the remover of all obstacles?	- Shri Ganesha
Name two ways to clear your Mooladhara chakra.	- Sit on the Mother Earth, footsoak
What is the name of Shri Ganesha's mouse?	- Mooshika
Who is Shri Ganesha's brother and what is His vahana?	- Shri Kartikeya with a peacock
What does Shri Ganesha hold in each of His four hands?	- A rope, a goad, sweets, and the fourth hand offers protection

MOOLADHARA CHAKRA (RIGHT)

TUESDAY

Right Mooladhara:	Shri Kartikeya
Vehicle:	Peacock
Country:	New Zealand
Location on hands:	Heel of the right palm
Cause of obstruction:	Rigid behavior
Qualities:	Dynamism, destuction of negative forces
Clearing:	"Shri Mataji, verily You are the killer of negativities.".

The Indian peacock has the brightest feathers in the bird kingdom. The long tail of an adult male is called a "train" and can reach 6 feet in length! The peacocks are among the largest of all birds that fly. (Ostriches, emus, and other such birds are bigger, but cannot fly.) The peacock is India's national bird.

Narakasura was an evil man (rakshasa), who lived on earth a long time ago. He was a power hungry king, cunning and treacherous, who brought all the kingdoms on earth under his control. Narakasura became the overlord of both Heaven and Earth. He tortured many people, and so many people prayed to Shri Shiva to free them of this evil man. Shri Shiva combined all the destructive powers to create Shri Kartikeya in order to kill the evil Narakasura. Shri Shiva then made Him the commander-in-chief of all the ganas.

Questions and Answers:

Who was Shri Gyaneshwara?	*- An incarnation of Shri Kartikeya*
Who is Shri Kartikeya's brother?	*- Shri Ganesha*
Why was Shri Kartikeya born?	*- To destroy evil Narakasura*
Who are Shri Kartikeya's parents?	*- Shri Shiva and Shri Parvati*

Shri Kartikeya is the destroyer of evil.

KUNDALINI

Deity: Shri Gauri
Element: Fire
Country: Maharashtra, India
Planet: Mother Earth
Qualities: Knowledge, love, compassion, attention

Kundalini means 'coiled energy' and refers to a power which lies in three and a half coils in the sacrum bone. It is a subtle power, a power of God's love.
To connect us to this subtle energy which permeates into every atom and molecule, there is a power of pure desire within us called as Kundalini. When the Kundalini is awakened it connects us to the all-pervading power (paramachaitanya).

— Shri Mataji Nirmala Devi

Kundalini is a primordial energy (an energy existing since the beginning of time) within us. This energy has many individual strands. It is like a rope and these strands are all twisted together to form the Kundalini. When the Kundalini rises, one or two strands out of this rope come up and pierce the fontanelle bone area (the Sahasrara) – only one or two. Kundalini is a spiral and travels upward on Brahma nadi (the central channel). Through the Brahma nadi, She starts sending those threads to the Sahasrara chakra.

— Shri Mataji Nirmala Devi

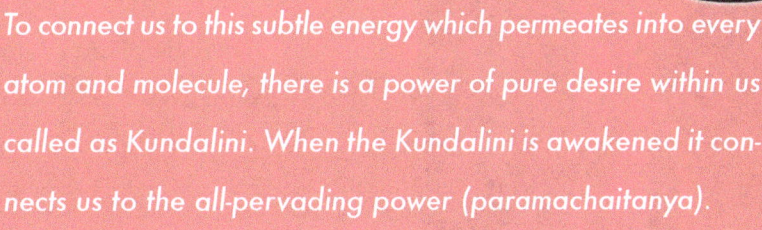

It is very interesting how the power of fire become the cool breeze.

Kundalini rises higher and higher because it is like fire. Fire never burns downward. It always burns upward. The Kundalini, just like the fire, has a capacity to purify, and to burn off that which is impure. It purifies things which it cannot burn and burns all the things which are flammable, which can be burnt out. This burning is so beautiful that it burns off all that is bad, stagnating, polluting, all diseases, and cools down the system.

It is very interesting to see how this power of fire becomes the cool breeze.

— Shri Mataji Nirmala Devi

What is Kundalini?

"We know of many energies such as electricity, light, heat, sound and many more. These energies cannot think, they cannot adjust, they cannot work on their own. They are to be handled by human beings. The Kundalini energy is different. It is a living energy and knows how to handle itself. It thinks! It works against gravity, because it has to rise to the fontanelle bone area at the top of the head. When Kundalini is awakened then whatever chakra She touches on it's way to Sahasrara chakra, She knows what is wrong with that chakra and starts fixing it. Kundalini, which is your individual Mother, is there to nourish you and look after you."

- Shri Mataji Nirmala Devi

Miracle photo of vibrations.

Kundalini means 'coiled energy' and it is a power which lies in three and a half coils in the sacrum bone.

"This energy is sleeping in the sacrum bone. When awakened it's a living process just like a seed sprouts - this Kundalini gets awakened, passes through six centers, and when it pierces through the last one you yourself feel the cool breeze coming out of your head. For the first time you start feeling the cool breeze. It is very pleasantly cool. This is the all-pervading power of divine love. With this you become like a divine computer. You can feel the centers which are in trouble within yourself. You can feel the centers of people around you. You can feel the centers of people who are far away, and also the centers of people who are dead and gone. That's how you can know who was a realized soul who came on this Earth."

- Shri Mataji Nirmala Devi

Kundalini is knowledge, love, compassion and attention.

The Kundalini energy is sleeping in the triangular bone area, waiting to be awakened.

"We are surrounded by divine power, and through the awakening of the Kundalini we get connected to this divine power. The Kundalini within you is your own mother, who brings you to the Kingdom of Heaven. The Kundalini is the ultimate desire to be one with the spirit (atma). Kundalini rises through the Sushumna nadi (the central channel). When the Kundalini crosses the door of

Agnya chakra, then you get into the state of thoughtless awareness. When she reaches the fontanelle bone area (the top of the head), you can feel the sound of your heart beating. Then, suddenly it stops and when it stops you start feeling the cool breeze coming out of your head (the chaitanya is the cool breeze of the Holy Ghost)."

- Shri Mataji Nirmala Devi

sacrum

The sacrum is a large triangular bone at the base of the lower spine.

On May 5th, 1970, Shri Mataji had opened the collective Sahasrara in Nargol, India.

"As soon as the Sahasrara was opened, the whole atmosphere was filled with tremendous chaitanya, and there was tremendous light in the sky, and the whole thing came on this earth, as if a torrential rain or a waterfall, with such tremendous force, as if I was unaware and got amazed. The happening was so tremendous and so unexpected, that I was stunned and got totally silent at the grandeur. I saw the primordial Kundalini rising like a big furnace, and the furnace was very silent but a burning appearance it had, as if you heat up a metal, and it had many colors. The same way, the Kundalini showed up like a furnace, like a tunnel. Then the deities came and sat on Their seats, Their golden seats."

"We have to respect all the people, all the human beings, whatever nation they come from, whatever country they belong to, whatever color they have, because they all have their Kundalini."

- Shri Mataji Nirmala Devi

Questions and Answers:

How many coils does the Kundalini have?	- Three and a half coils
Who protects the Kundalini?	- Shri Ganesha
Through which channel does the Kundalini rise?	- Through the central channel
What is the only force working against gravity?	- The Kundalini force
Before awakening, where does the Kundalini sleep?	- In the sacrum bone
What's another name for the central channel?	- The Sushumna nadi (central channel)

SWADHISTANA CHAKRA

WEDNESDAY

Deity:	Shri Brahmadeva, Shri Saraswati
Number of petals:	6
Body parts:	Liver, spleen, pancreas, kidney
Musical instrument:	Veena
Color:	Coral yellow
Element:	Fire
Country:	L - Africa, Nepal
	R - France
Vehicle:	Swan
Location on the hands:	Left and right thumb
Precious stone:	Amethyst
Symbol:	Star of David
Planet:	Mercury
Qualities:	Art, creativity, pure desire
Causes of obstruction:	Too much thinking and planning, bad eating habits (eating junk food), artificial behavior, drinking alcohol

Shri Saraswati and Lord Brahmadeva reside in the Swadhistana chakra. The Swadhistana chakra is the second chakra on the subtle system. The Swadhistana chakra is suspended like a satellite on a chord from the Nabhi chakra and moves around the Void area. It is a very important chakra: on the left side it creates all our desires, and the right channel starts on the level of the Swadhistana chakra. The main quality of this chakra is creativity, but this chakra also generates fat cells, that - upon reaching the brain - get converted into a power supply that helps the brain to think and process all information received.

The origin of all creativity is love. If there is no love there is no creativity.

Shri Saraswati teaches us through nature: listen to the sounds of birds, the gurgling of a creek or the thundering roar of a waterfall, the wind rustling through the leaves of a tree or blowing through the canyons with might. These are all Shri Saraswati's expressions. Look at the many shades of green in a garden, look at the sky and see Her paintings in the clouds, how many colors She uses when the sun rises over the ocean or sets over the mountains, and enjoy Her creation. Smell the fragrance of a rose bush, or the fresh resin of a tree, breathe in the scent of sandalwood or myrrh incense to strengthen your Mooladhara chakra. The whole creation of this earth and beyond has been made for us to enjoy.

The origin of all creativity is love. If there is no love there is no creativity. Shri Saraswati holds a veena, on which She plays the most beautiful music to inspire all the people. Shri Saraswati teaches us not only beautiful music, but also how to dance, speak, sing, write books, to paint and to build. When we meditate, She gives us access to all the knowledge we can hold.

Sahaja yogis performing to please Shri Mataji.

Shri Saraswati gives us pure knowledge on the left side and balance on the right side.

"When the Kundalini nourishes this center, people become extremely creative. Once you get your self-realization the Kundalini clears you. Now you have seen these artists who are playing here. They were very simple, ordinary artists, but after coming to Sahaja Yoga suddenly they have bloomed so much."

- Shri Mataji Nirmala Devi

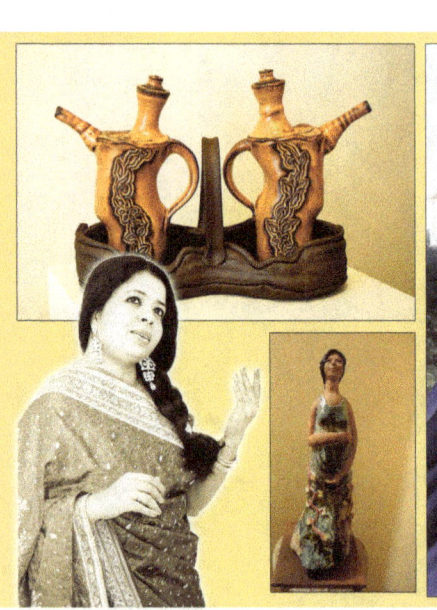

"So far we have never worshiped Saraswati. Brahmadeva is not worshiped anywhere, because He created this world, He created all these woods and all these things, and He created all the seas and all the lands, all the stars, universes after universes. But we are not to worship like we worship this tree or that tree. We are not to worship anything of that kind, only thing, whatever is created by Mother Earth like swayambhus. Brahmadeva created human beings to evolve and then ultimately lead them to Shiva."

Amethyst

- Shri Mataji Nirmala Devi

The brain is the Virat, the heart is Shiva, and the liver is Brahmadeva.

"Art is such that it should stop your thoughts. The art that we appreciate should give vibrations. All the great paintings, all the great creative works of the world have vibrations. All the art work that has vibrations has been sustained by time. All the work that does not have vibrations gets destroyed by nature and is forgotten over time. Italians are known for their art, they make beautiful things."
- Shri Mataji Nirmala Devi

Albert Einstein   Mona Lisa painting by Leonardo Da Vinci   Michelangelo Sistene Chapel painting

Some of the realized artists in the past were:

William Shakespeare (poet), Michelangelo (painter), Albert Einstein (scientist), Leonardo Da Vinci (painter), Abraham Lincoln (politician), William Blake (poet), Mozart (musician) and many more.

Questions and Answers:

Who is the goddess of art and learning?	- Shri Saraswati
What animal is the vehicle of Shri Brahmadeva and Shri Saraswati?	- A swan
What instrument does Shri Saraswati play?	- The veena
How many petals does the Swadhistana have?	- 6
What element represents the Swadhistana chakra?	- Fire
What planet does the Swadhistana chakra represent?	- Mercury
Name two famous realized people.	- Einstein, Michelangelo..
What is the main quality of the Swadhistana chakra?	- Creativity
What color is the Swadhistana chakra?	- Yellow
What country represents the Swadhistana chakra?	- Africa
	L - South Africa
	R - Germany

4 - The Man-Lion

3 - The Boar

2 - The Turtle

5 - The Short Man

1 - The Fish

6 - Shri Parashurama

7 - Shri Ram

8 - Shri Krishna

9 - Jesus Christ

10 - Shri Kalki

NABHI CHAKRA

THURSDAY

What stone am I? (dlaremE)

Deities:	Shri Lakshmi, Shri Vishnu
Left:	Shri Gruha Lakshmi
Right:	Shri Raja Lakshmi
Number of petals:	10 Petals
Body parts:	Stomach, liver
Musical insturment:	Santoor
Color:	Green
Element:	Water
Countries:	Europe, Greece
	L - Austria, the Netherlands
	R - France, Switzerland
Vehicle:	Eagle Garuda
Location on the hands:	Middle fingers
Precious stone:	Emerald
Symbol:	Yin Yang
Planet:	Jupiter
Qualities:	Satisfaction, peace, dharma, evolution, self mastery in dealing with the material world
Causes of obstruction:	Fasting, family and household problems, worrying, food that is bad for the liver (junk food), anger and bad temper
Clearing:	"Mother, please, make me satisfied." Before eating, give vibrations to all the food and drinks.

Shri Vishnu sleeps on the magnificent cosmic serpent Vasuki, whose body is His couch and whose seven hooded jeweled heads are His canopy on the cosmic waters.

Shri Lakshmi is his wife. Her beautiful skin has the color of gold with a sheen of pearls. Her black hair rolls down in waves to Her knees. Her eyes look like lotuses, peaceful, calm and steady. She stands on a pink lotus. She was born from the sea during the great churning where the snake Vasuki was used as a rope during the churning of the ocean.

The Nabhi chakra is made of water.

Shri Lakshmi is the goddess, who stands on the lotus. She shows that a wealthy person has to be someone who does not push people around but rather should be someone who is balanced. Shri Lakshmi is a lady. She is a mother. She is peace.

Shri Vishnu with His power Shri Lakshmi resides in our Nabhi chakra. He rules the Sushumna nadi (the central channel). All the chakras are placed in the Sushumna, and it is He who controls the chakras with His various forms and powers. To develop Shri Vishnu's qualities, one needs to stay responsible and balanced. From time to time He and His wife descends upon the earth, in animal or human forms, with the purpose of saving the world from increasing evil.

The 10 Incarnations of Shri Vishnu

1 - **The Fish (Matsya)** - Born to save people from the great flood.

2 - **The Tortoise (Kurma)** - Born to help the Devas in churning the ocean to obtain the amrut.

3 - **The Boar (Varaha)** - Born to retrieve the Earth and the Vedas from the demon Hiranyakashipu.

4 - **The Man-Lion (Narasimha)** - Born to destroy the demon Hiranyakashipu.

5 - **The Short Man (Vamana)** - the one who measured the world with three steps.

6 - **Shri Parashurama** - Born to punish the arrogance of wayward kings and to re-establish dharma among men.

7 - **Shri Rama** - The ideal king and human being who was born to establish the maryadas.

8 - **Shri Krishna** - Born to free humanity from religious ritualism.

9 - **Lord Jesus Christ** - Born to open the Agnya chakra.

10 - **Shri Kalki** - The rider of the last days of Kali-Yuga, deity of the Sahasrara chakra.

"White rice, yogurt, cooked fresh vegetables, some chicken, and fruits are all good for cooling and clearing the liver. White cane sugar, taken in liquid form, works as a detergent for a hot liver. It is rare to find a person with a liver that is too cold, but in that case, he should eat yellow vegetables. For liver problems of all types, one should drink several quarts of water every day which helps flush away toxins."

- *Shri Mataji Nirmala Devi*

How to care for a hot liver!

The Nabhi chakra is also responsible for our liver. A healthy, cool liver gives us good concentration and attention. It is important to take care of our liver by following a good diet, and keep it from overheating. If we think or plan too much, our liver will heat up too.

Shri Vishnu flies on the eagle Garuda.

Satisfaction is the key quality of the Nabhi chakra.

The Nabhi chakra has three parts: the left, the right, and the center. On the left hand side is the Gruha Lakshmi (wife), on the right hand side is the Raja Lakshmi or Gaja Lakshmi (queen), and in the center is the Lakshmi which ascends into Mahalakshmi.

In day to day life, when we are blessed with the qualities of Shri Lakshmi, we find we are helped to move around, we have sufficient prosperity to enjoy our generosity, and we always have transport and people around to help us when needed while doing Shri Mataji'a work.

> *The churning of the Cosmic Ocean took place in order to obtain amrita - the nectar of immortal life. At the suggestion of Vishnu, the gods, (devas) and demons (asuras) churned the ocean in order to obtain amrita which guaranteed them immortality. To churn the ocean they used the Serpent King, Vasuki, for their churning-rope. For a churning pole they used Mount Mandara placed on the back of the Great Tortoise - the Kurma Avatar of Vishnu. When the amrita finally emerged, along with several other treasures, the devas and asuras fought over it. However, Vishnu in the form of Mohini, the enchantress, managed to lure the asuras into handing over the amrita to Her, which She then distributed to only the devas.*

What is Dharma? Another aspect of the Nabhi chakra is that of dharma or the moral conduct in our lives. Dharma protects and nourishes our spiritual growth. The ten commandments brought down from Mount Sinai by Moses are the 10 principles of dharma to guide us.

Mount Sinai was covered by the a cloud for six days, after which Moses went into the midst of the cloud and stayed on the mount for forty days and forty nights. He received two stone tablets from God.

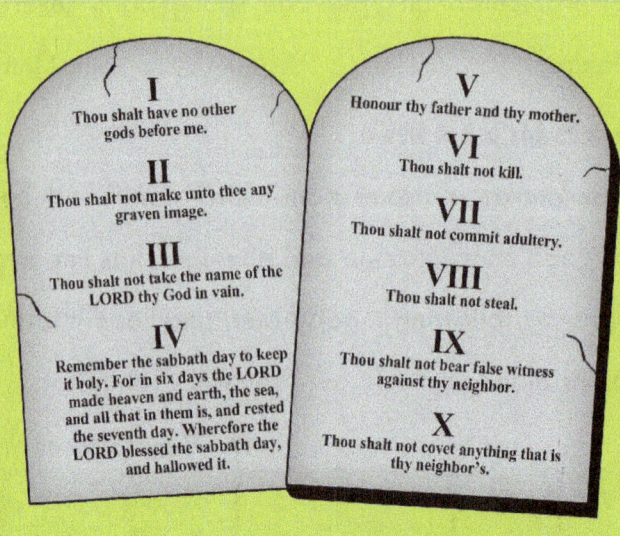

"This center controls the working of the stomach area. The stomach is very important and if its functioning gets disturbed, then the process of digestion of food is affected. If we are in a hurry or angry or worried when eating, then the food will not be properly digested because the stomach muscles are tensed and cannot work properly. For proper nourishment, eating peacefully is a must - it should be a meditation. Fasting or thinking too much about food negatively affects the Nabhi chakra. It keeps the stomach excited and blocks the energy flow."

- Shri Mataji Nirmala

Jupiter is the fifth planet from the sun and the largest planet in the solar system. It is a gas giant. The best known feature of Jupiter is the Great Red Spot, a persistent anticyclonic storm that is larger than Earth. It has been suggested that the storm is stable and may be a permanent feature of the planet. Storms on Jupiter can last as little as a few hours or stretch on for centuries.

Questions and Answers:

Who dwells on the right and left Nabhi? - Shri Raja Lakshmi - R
  - Shri Gruha Lakshmi - L

What is dharma? - Moral behavior

How many petals does the Nabhi chakra have? - 10

What is the name of Shri Vishnu's eagle? - Garuda

What planet represents the Nabhi chakra? - Jupiter

What is the symbol of the Nabhi chakra? - Yin Yang

Name at least 5 incarnations of Shri Vishnu. - The Fish, the Tortoise, the Boar, the Man-Lion, the Dwarf, Parashurama, Shri Rama, Shri Krishna, Lord Jesus Christ, Shri Kalki

VOID

Deity:	Shri Adi Guru Dattatreya
Element:	All the elements
Companion:	Dog (as the perfect disciple)
Location on hands:	Base of fingers and outer ring of palm
Country:	Middle East: Egypt, Iran, Turkey, Iraq, Yemen, Saudi Arabia, Syria, Israel, Jordan, Kuwait, Cyprus, Qatar, Bahrain, Palestine, Lebanon, United Arab Emirates, Oman
Qualities:	Gravity, leadership
Causes of obstruction:	False knowledge, false gurus, black magic, fanaticism
Clearing:	"Shri Mataji, please, make me my own guru/master."

"Around the Nabhi chakra is the Bhav Sagar, the Ocean of Illusions, also called as Void (void means gap). The job of a guru (teacher) is to transform an ordinary human being into a higher personality out of an ordinary human being through love and compassion. The key to becoming a guru is patience, complete patience, and complete dependency on God Almighty. At that state you start controlling all the elements."
— Shri Mataji Nirmala Devi

My desire is only one and that is that you all should become gurus yourself.
- Shri Mataji Nirmala Devi

"To act as a guru you should know all about Sahaja Yoga, the theory and the practice of it, then you can become a guru. You should not have any ego, first, you should not have any of your chakras catching; you should be absolutely clear all the time and the vibrations should be flowing in both the hands. So you have to be a perfect Sahaja yogi. I can't travel from places to places all the time, so you have to do My job. You have to be able to give en-masse realization. If you can give en-masse realization then you could be a guru. You can use My photograph but the realization should not be from the photograph, but from you."
— Shri Mataji Nirmala Devi

Raja Janaka was Shri Sita's father. Shri Rama won Shri Sita's hand by being able to string the bow of Shri Shiva.

German Spitz

*Dogs are the vehicle of the guru tattwa.
(The master/disciple principle)*

Shri Mataji talking about Her Dog Deepak:

"I have a dog too. It is with My daughter now. When I go to India, when I go to My daughter's place, I wear a very ordinary saree, because I know, as soon as My dog hears My voice, he comes running and jumps all over Me. He licks Me and also shows his anger, because I have left him. His eyes will have tears. And when I am coming and filling My bag, then he goes and sits and sulks, and does not eat food for eight days. I mean, I go every second year, but he does not forget My voice. His name is Deepak, means the light. He is absolutely white, is a spitz from Germany. Dogs have a capacity to love. He has learned to discriminate even the footsteps of every person in the house. And he never liked nudity of any kind. One Yugoslav lady came wearing shorts, her legs were showing, and my dog started barking at her. So I had to give a towel to cover her legs, while she was talking to me.

In India men wear dhotis, and if they were to show their knees, he would not like it, so they had to cover for him.

He would bark at paintings, and he could not bear any sleeveless clothes, or these translucent dresses people wear. He was very particular, very kind to children.

But my dog has the vibrations and such a sense of respect and protocol. And he himself, you know, if anything is given to him with love he would eat, otherwise he will not. He is the vehicle of the guru tattwa, the master principle, so the disciples are the vehicle of a guru. You have to be able to bear my powers, otherwise my powers are useless."

- Shri Mataji Nirmala Devi

10 Primordial Masters are:

Raja Janaka - India 5000 BC

Abraham - Mesopotamia, Palestine, 2000 BC

Moses - Palestine, Egypt region 1200 BC,

Zarathustra - Persia, 1000 BC

Confucius - China, 551 - 579 BC

Lao-Tsu - China, 6th century BC

Socrates - Athens, Greece, 469 - 399 BC

Prophet Muhammad - Mecca, Arabia, 570 - 632 AD

Guru Nanak - Punjab, India, 1469 - 1539

Shri Sai Baba of Shirdi - India, 1838 - 1918 AD

Raja Janaka   Abraham   Moses   Zarathustra   Confucius

Lao-Tsu   Socrates   Prophet Muhammad   Guru Nanaka   Shri Sai Baba of Shirdi

"The primordial Guru always has a dog accompanying Him. Dogs only know and obey one master. The dog reflects the disciple principle of the guru tattwa. So the disciple principle is like a dog, who guards the guru, who shows complete devotion and dedication and is all the time on the watch that the wrong type of people should not come to the guru."

— Shri Mataji Nirmala Devi

Questions and Answers:

Which guru had miraculously parted the sea?	- Moses
Which guru was the father of Shri Sita?	- Raja Janaka
What animal is the companion of Shri Adi Guru Dattatreya?	- A dog
Name all 10 incarnations of Adi Guru Dattatreya.	- Raja Janaka, Abraham, Moses, Zarathustra, Confucius, Lao-Tsu, Socrates, Prophet Muhammad, Guru Nanak, Shri Sai Baba of Shridi

A dog knows what pleases the guru, and as soon as the guru comes home, he will express all his joy. He will give up everything and run to express his joy. They are wonderful things, they are beautiful.

— *Shri Mataji Nirmala Devi*

ANAHATA CHAKRA (CENTER)

FRIDAY

Deities:	Shri Durga, Shri Jagadamba
Left heart:	Shri Shiva & Shri Parvati
Right heart:	Shri Sita & Shri Ram
Number of petals:	12 petals
Body parts and functions:	Sternum bone and antibody production, lungs
Flower:	Lotus
Musical instrument:	Tabla
Color:	Ruby red
Element:	Air
Countries:	Calcutta, Ireland
Vehicle:	Tigers and lions
Location on the hands:	Little fingers
Precious stone:	Ruby
Symbol:	Flame
Astral connection:	Venus
Qualities:	Love, security, compassion, confidence
Cause of obstruction:	Fear
Clearing:	"Shri Mataji, please, make me fearless." Give vibrations to your heart, from the front and back.

Shri Durga is the ruling deity of our center heart chakra. She is a mother who is extremely gentle and kind to Her children but fierce and terrifying when She faces negative forces trying to harm Her children. She rides a lion (and tiger too) to destroy fears. These wild animals are under Her complete control.

What country flag am I? (dnalgnE)

England is the heart of the universe.

"Those who do not have their central heart properly developed suffer from tremendous insecurity all their lives. When the antibodies, that are built in the body, are not sufficient in number, this center becomes weak. The heart has to pump. It has to be strong! So you have to have a lion's heart. And lion's heart means he is not afraid. He is the king. He knows he's the king and he lives like a king. There should be no fear. So if your heart is weak, the Kundalini cannot pierce through. So by placing Me in your heart and by raising Me to your Sahasrara, you can cure your heart."

- *Shri Mataji Nirmala Devi*

Just try to put Me in your heart; is very simple. "Mother, please, be in my heart".
- *Shri Mataji Nirmala Devi*

The ganas, also called the **antibodies,** are situated in the sternum bone, where they are produced, and fight off attacks and diseases. The antibodies are under the control of the center heart chakra. **Intuition** is nothing but the help of the ganas which are surrounding us. When a person learns to take help from the ganas, such person becomes intuitive.

"Joan of Arc" was a specially blessed person by the Divine.

Back in the days when Mahishasura was the lord of the asuras (demons), Indra was the lord of the devas. There was a terrible battle waged for 100 years. The asuras drove the devas out of Heaven and Mahishasura became the lord of the three worlds. The devas led by Brahmadeva, went to seek protection and help from Shri Shiva and Shri Vishnu. After hearing about the evil doings of Mahishasura and his army, Shri Brahmadeva, Shri Shiva and Shri Vishnu became very angry.

A great divine light came out from their faces. More lights sprung from Indra and the other assembled devas too. All these lights joined together in a blinding radiance penetrating every corner of the three worlds with its brilliance. From this mass of light there appeared a female form shining brighter than the sun - Shri Durga. Upon seeing Her, all the devas were full of joy. Then, one by one, the gods came forth to give Her weapons and ornaments. Shri Shiva gave Her a trident, Shri Vishnu a discus, Shri Brahmadeva gave Her a water pot filled with

Tigers and lions are the largest living cats. Lions are considered the kings of all animals.

All the lions and tigers of the world protect Sahaja Yogis.

holy water, which when sprinkled on asuric (demonic) forces removed their bravery. Shri Kubera, the god of wealth, gifted a club. Indra, the lord of Heaven, gifted a thunderbolt born out of his own thunderbolt. Kaala, the God of time gave Her a sword. Vayu, the Wind God gifted a bow and Surya, the God of the Sun, gifted arrows.

Himavat the father of Parvati and lord of the Himalayas offered Her a lion. The ocean presented Shri Durga with a lotus flower representing purity.

These days we can't see Shri Durga riding a lion and killing asuras. Everything has become more subtle, but Shri Durga exists in the hearts of every Sahaja yogi, as security and love. When we are troubled by infections, Shri Durga sends antibodies (ganas) out to fight the invading forces and when we are troubled by fear we need only take a mantra and she fills our hearts with courage.

Shri Durga destroyed Mahishasura and his army in a battle lasting 9 days. These 9 days of battle are called **Navaratri**.

Venus is the second planet from the Sun. Venus is sometimes called Earth's "sister planet" because of their similar size and gravity. Venus is by far the hottest planet in the Solar System. Venus has several times as many volcanoes as Earth, and it possesses 167 large volcanoes. Much of the Venusian surface appears to have been shaped by volcanic activity.

Questions and Answers:

What country is the heart of the universe?	- England
What is the name of the mother of the universe?	- Shri Jagadamba
What musical instrument cleanses the heart chakra?	- The tabla
What planet represents the heart chakra?	- Venus
Shri Durga rides on what animal?	- Tigers and lions
What are antibodies?	- They are ganas
What stone represents the heart chakra?	- The ruby
Who is the deity of the central heart?	- Shri Durga, Shri Jagadamba
What are the qualities of the heart chakra?	- Love, security, compassion, confidence
What is Navaratri?	- A festival celebrating a battle that lasted 9 full days, where Shri Durga destroyed all evil on earth.

tabla

ANAHATA CHAKRA (LEFT)

FRIDAY

Deities:	Shri Shiva, Shri Parvati
Body parts:	Solar plexus
Countries:	England
	Spain - atma (the spirit)
	Italy - jivatma (the soul)
Vehicle:	Bull Nandi
Location on the hands:	Left little finger
Qualities:	Joy of the spirit
Causes of obstruction:	Roving eyes, bad company
Clearing:	"Shri Mataji, by Your grace, I am the spirit."
	"Shri Mataji, by Your grace, please forgive me for any mistakes against my spirit.

Shri Mataji talking about Tad Nishkala: "You are eternal bliss and awareness, consciousness: the pure consciousness. Everyone must learn it by heart, and you must say it in all the ashrams. That's a very good way of remembering what you are."

Shri Shiva and His wife Shri Parvati live on the snowy peaks of Mount Kailash. They have two children, Shri Ganesha and Shri Kartikeya. Shri Shiva's sister is Shri Saraswati. When Shri Shiva becomes furious with the evil forces, He performs His celestial dance (Nataraja) and it is said to cause the movement of the universe. Shri Shiva creates, preserves and destroys. Shri Shiva is also the lord of goblins, demons and restless spirits, because He loves all the creation. He rides Nandi, the snow-white bull, son of Surabhi. (The ocean's first gift was the divine cow Surabhi.)

Nataraja, Shri Shiva's celestial dance.

The goal of our life is to become the spirit.

Shri Shiva holds a trident in His lower right, which represents the three powers within us (rajo, tamo, satwa). The river Ganges starts in the knot of His hair, flowing down to Earth. The cobra around His neck is called Naagraj and shows that ego, once mastered, can be worn as an ornament. The moon on His forehead symbolizes that Shri Shiva is the master of time; He is beyond time.

The bindi on His forehead is the eye of knowledge (third eye), which, if opened, burns to ashes anyone in it's vision. It is a symbol of the destruction of evil. Shri Shiva wearing a tiger skin shows how fearless Shri Shiva is. The drum symbolizes the sound of the heart beat, the melody without percussion (Anahat). Shri Shiva drank the Halahala poison churned up from the ocean to eliminate its destructive capacity and to save the world from its poisoning. However the poison was so potent that it colored His neck blue.

Shri Shiva is the guru... Shri Parvati is the shakti.

Mount Kailash

Shri Shiva is the destroyer of all negative forces. His destruction has already started and is going with full speed. He destroys negative forces with the help of hurricanes, storms and earthquakes. At the same time there is another force at work: Shri Shiva resurrects people. He teaches people how to become the spirit, the Self. When Sahaja yogis meditate and keep themselves in complete peace and surrender, nothing can happen to them, nothing can hurt them. They will always be saved, they are under the complete protection of their Mother.

Shri Parvati Herself wanted to have a child of Her own. There were angels who were dedicated either to Shri Vishnu or to Shri Shiva, like ganas were dedicated to Shri Shiva alone. So, She wanted to have Her own son, who could permeate Her powers on Earth. The first thing She created was innocence, and the embodiment of that innocence was Shri Ganesha.

The Heart Chakra is located behind the sternum bone. In the sternum bone the antibodies (ganas) are produced to protect us against diseases and any form of negativity. When this chakra is clear, we become absolutely fearless, strong and loving. The spirit lives in our left heart.

"All that is, what today you have to give Me, a promise that, whenever you meet any other human being, you will tell them about Sahaja Yoga. Not that it's important, but it is an absolutely immediate need of the world. If you understand this point, that at this time, why are you in this world and what is the need of the world, you will immediately start feeling the responsibility. Whether you are a man or a woman is not important. Go all out to preach, think, make people understand about Sahaja Yoga in every way that is possible."

- Shri Mataji Nirmala Devi

The ocean's first gift was the divine cow Surabhi.

Shri Shiva is the guru, He is the one who is our guru.

The spirit is the Holy Ghost, and the spirit is in the heart. The spirit is the reflection of God within us. It is a live force. It is your spirit which is going to guide you, so if you want to develop the strength of your spirit, you have to listen to it. You can maneuver the Kundalini, but not the spirit. You can raise your hand, the Kundalini will move, you can give it a bandhan, it will go round and round, but what about the spirit? You have to bring the Kundalini to look after it, you have to take the Kundalini to your left heart.

One has to follow what the heart says, not the brain. And the more you open on your vibrations, the more you use your heart, your spirit. If you can just leave things to your heart to work it out, and don't think. Pay attention to your heart and let the spirit emit itself.

- Shri Mataji Nirmala Devi

Shiva represents the spirit, and the spirit is residing in all of you in your hearts. The seat of Sadashiva is on top of your head; but He's reflected in your heart. Now, your brain is the Vitthala. So to bring the spirit to your brain.

Questions and Answers:

What country is the spirit?	- Spain
What deity controls the left heart?	- Shri Shiva & Shri Parvati
Where does the spirit reside in our body?	- In the left heart
What is the Tandav?	- Dance of destruction of Shri Shiva
What is the name of the snake around Shri Shiva's neck?	- Naagraj
What are ganas?	- The soldiers of Shri Shiva's army
What is the responsibility of the Sahaja yogis?	- To give self-realization
Where do Shri Shiva and Shri Parvati live?	- On Mount Kailash
What is the name of Shri Shiva's vehicle?	- The bull Nandi
Why did Shri Shiva's neck turn blue?	- Because he drank the Halahal poison

ANAHATA CHAKRA (RIGHT)

FRIDAY

Deities:	Shri Sita, Shri Rama
Country:	Germany, Japan
Location on the hands:	Little finger on the right hand
Qualities:	Responsible behaviour
Causes of obstruction:	Arrogant behavior, emotional aggression
Clearing:	"Shri Mataji, you are the responsibility in me." Give vibrations to your right heart and put an icepack on your liver to cool down.

"Shri Rama was full of grace, a formal person. He would go to any extend to bear upon Himself problems, rather then telling others to do something. This was His greatest quality - He would not order anyone to do anything for him."
- Shri Mataji Nirmala Devi

Shri Rama and His wife Shri Sita rule the right side of the heart. Shri Rama was the ideal human being, perfect king, son, father, brother, husband and man. He was an example of truthfulness and sacrifice.

Raja Janaka was the king of Mithila and the father of Shri Sita. One day He proposed a test of strength in which suitors vying for His daughter's hand in marriage would have to string the great bow of Shri Shiva, which was very big and heavy. Shri Rama passed this test, and got to marry Shri Sita. Shri Rama's shakti (power) was his wife Shri Sita, who was a very dignified and humble queen. She was also an incarnation of the Adi Shakti.

- Shri Mataji Nirmala Devi

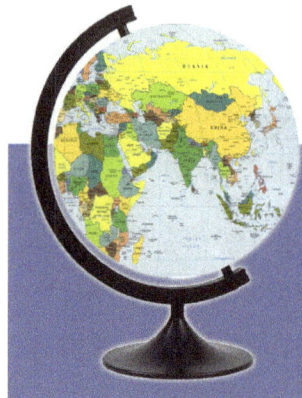

He is the father, He is the father king, and He is the father of this world.

The word 'Diwali' comes from 'deepa wali', means the 'festival of lights'. It was celebrated firstly because thousands of years back Shri Rama was crowned to be a king on this day. That means the benevolence of a human being was crowned, was accepted. And in Shri Rama's life you see an ideal personality being shown to be a king, to be the benevolent king as described by Socrates. So this was a great, joyous thing, that a benevolent king was crowned. That means, we have to have a king, who is benevolent. That's only possible if the people, who choose the king, have no other consideration but that of benevolence of all the people.

The monkey army building a bridge to Lanka. Shri Hanuman bringing a mountain to Shri Rama.

The Story of the Ramayana

Rama, Sita, and Lakshama were exiled into the wilderness for fourteen years. They journeyed southward along the banks of river Godavari, where they built cottages and lived a simple life off of the land.

While in the forest, the demon king Ravana kidnapped Sita. Ravana took Sita to his evil kingdom of Lanka. Rama and Lakshmana went in search of Sita and entered the kingdom of monkeys. Rama and Lakshmana met Hanumana, who was very strong and brave. Rama and Lakshman asked Hanumana to help them find Sita. In Their search of Sita, They came to the shores of a vast ocean and looked across. Ravana's evil kingdom of Lanka was on an island far into the ocean. Hanumana leaped across to meet Sita and tell Her that Rama was coming for Her. Later, He burned the entire island of Lanka to ashes, in order to warn Ravana that Rama had arrived. But, by magic, the city rose up again the next day morning.

To get across the ocean, the monkey army built the raised bridge across the ocean into Lanka. They all marched across. At Lanka, Ravana's army fought Rama's army. Rama defeated Ravana and rescued Sita. Rama, Sita, Lakshmana, Hanumana, and all the monkeys went back to Ayodhya. The people of Ayodhya were thrilled to see them. Rama was made the king of Ayodhya and Sita the queen.

This day is called as Diwali.

Shri Rama was the 7th incarnation of Shri Vishnu.

"You have to be human beings of a very great quality. You have to be people who have created new worlds. You are going to be that, I know. You have to just rise up to that point." - Shri Mataji Nirmala Devi

"I had awakened Hanumana and Shri Rama within you, but keep them awake. Keep them alert, and you have to be alert and active, responsible and respectable. You have to realize that you are saints, saints of a very special quality, the saints who can give realization to others. There has been nothing done like this before. Today there are saints who are realized souls but they don't know how to give realization. They don't know as much as you do about the Kundalini and the subtle system. And that is how you must know that within you Hanumana and Shri Rama have awakened, keep it awake, keep it alert.

- Shri Mataji Nirmala Devi

"Shri Rama was the ideal that came on this earth to teach us how to be responsible, respectful and understanding of others. He went to such an extent that He had to sacrifice His own wife, Shri Sita, for the sake of the state. He had to ask His wife, who was pregnant, to go and live with a very great sage. She was the Goddess. Shri Rama, understood the responsibility He had as a king, and the responsibility He had towards others as well as towards Himself. This feeling of responsibility is lacking in us, however. In our own life, we should ask ourselves, "Are we responsible"? People have the problem of the right side. To worship the right side, we have to see to Shri Rama. How He felt responsible for the whole world. How He used to look after people. How He looked after the things of other people. How He behaved towards other people. That's a very important thing, which we have to learn. He would not do anything to disturb another person. As far as possible, He would try to console and have the formalities of good living. Formality is meant for good living and good understanding. The feeling of responsibility can be built up only when you know about Shri Rama's life, the way He led His life. You have to feel responsible in every way of life."

- Shri Mataji Nirmala Devi

Shri Rama would go to any extent to bear problems Himself, rather then telling others to do something.

A bridge discovered by NASA, believed to be the bridge built by Shri Rama's army thousands of years ago.

Questions and Answers:

On what festival do we light deepas? — Diwali

Why is Diwali celebrated? — It was a day when Shri Rama was coronated

What is the Ramayana? — The life story of Shri Rama, Shri Sita and Shri Lakshmana

Who was Shri Sita's father? — Raja Janaka

What is Shri Rama's message to us? — To take on our responsibilities

Shri Sita & Shri Rama had two sons, what are their names? — Luv, Khush

Who was Laksmana? — Shri Rama's brother

What countries represent the right heart? — Japan, Germany

VISHUDDHI CHAKRA

Deities:	Shri Radha, Shri Krishna
Left Vishuddhi:	Shri Vishnumaya
Right Vishuddhi:	Shri Yeshoda
Number of petals:	16
Chakra controls:	Neck, arms, ankles, wrists, teeth, nose, ears, mouth, face, speech, eye movement
Musical instrument:	Flute
Color:	Blue
Shri Krishan's favorite food:	Butter
Element:	Ether
Countries:	North, Central and South America Scandinavian countries, some Eastern European countries
Location on the hands:	Both index fingers
Precious stone:	Sapphire
Symbol:	Time wheel
Astral connection:	Saturn
Qualities:	Respect for self and others, diplomatic sweet communication, innocent playfulness
Causes of obstruction:	Bad language (swearing), smoking, feeling guilty
Clearing:	Say "Allah hu Akbar" 16 times, use ajwan dhuni, keep your teeth and mouth clean.

On the day Shri Krishna was born, His sister Shri Vishnumaya announced by lightening, that the Lord had incarnated! It was a stormy night, and His father carried Him in a basket on his head and walked through a flooded river to get to their village.

Shri Krishna grew up in a small village called Vrindavan. Little Shri Krishna loved butter. He would play tricks to get the butter, no matter how His mother and the other gopis tried to hide it. Shri Krishna's mother, Shri Yeshoda, had enough of little Krishna's tricks to get butter. One day She found Him with butter on His face. "Open your mouth and show Me what is inside!" She demanded. When He opened His mouth, Shri Yeshoda saw the entire universe inside! She realized that Her little son was actually the lord of the universe.

Saturn has the most spectacular ring system of all our solar system's planets. It is made up of seven rings with several gaps and divisions between them.

Saturn by Hubble telescope.

One day the villagers found a huge snake in their river Yamuna. This was not just a snake, it was the evil Kaliya with a hundred heads. He made the water poisonous so it would kill all animals and plants nearby. One day little Krishna went in the river, Kaliya reared up and grabbed him and tried to kill him. Shri Krishna jumped up onto the snake's

head and began playing His flute and dancing. As He stomped His feet on the snake's ego, Kaliya was humbled. Kaliya asked for forgiveness and promised Shri Krishna that He would not bother anyone ever again.

Today Shri Krishna lives in our Vishuddhi chakras. He helps us to speak sweetly, and He shows us how to love our brothers and sisters. He helps us not to be bothered and react, when people do things that we don't like. And He helps us to enjoy the trees, the animals, the sky... everything.

Collectivity is one of the qualities of the Vishuddhi Chakra.

Where is the Vishuddhi Chakra ?

The Vishuddhi is located at the base of the neck. This chakra controls many parts of the body such as the ears, eyes, nose, neck, throat, face, cheeks, teeth, skin and much more. In the Vishuddhi chakra we develop our sense of collectivity and how to sweetly communicate with each other. This chakra is very important, and all the Sahaja yogis in North and South America are responsible for the Vishuddhi of the whole world.

The Vishuddhi chakra picks up on the etheric vibrations from wherever we place our attention. This is a very good reason to be careful where and how we place our attention. The Vishuddhi is the flute, which expresses the sweetness of the heart.

Shri Krishna was a diplomat and master of speech. He praised instead of criticizing and showed respect to all people. His speech was never harsh or sarcastic, but soft and sweet. Shri Krishna's sister is Shri Vishnumaya, who protects our left Vishuddhi and helps us not to feel guilty.

We should not feel guilty, but learn from our mistakes instead.

When the Vishuddhi chakra catches, we stop feeling vibrations in our hands.

"At the time when Shri Krishna came, people were serious and had become very ritualistic. They had lost the sense of joy and beauty. Shri Krishna thought that there should be a way by which people should be able to laugh freely and be joyful. So He started a nice childlike play called Holi, where people dance and sing together. Holi is a festival of colors (celebrated mid March in India). It celebrates the triumph of good over evil."

- Shri Mataji Nirmala Devi

"We should try to never say anything harsh which might hurt another person. Otherwise this anger will make us catch on the left Vishuddhi, bacause we start feeling guilty for what we have said. There is no need for any temper if we are masters. If we find we have anger we should watch out. It starts from the liver and expresses through the Vishuddhi. To master anger, one has to face himself and become a witness."

- Shri Mataji Nirmala Devi

Shri Krishna has given us certain limits and relationships such as the sweet relationship between a brother and a sister. The special nature of this love of brother and sister is born by nature. This behavior is called MARYADAS.

Humor should not be sarcastic. Sarcasm damages our Vishuddhi chakra.

What is Rakshabandhan?

It is an occasion where a sister ties a rakhi thread (which comes in many colors and designs) on the wrist of her brother. The brother in return offers a gift to his sister. When a boy becomes a brother, he must protect his sister at all times against all negative forces. The rakhi thread is a symbol of respect and love between brothers and sisters.

Questions and Answers:

What was the name of the snake Shri Krishna fought?	- *Kaliya*
Who is Shri Krisna's sister?	- *Shri Vishnumaya*
What is a rakhi?	- *A thread that sisters tie onto to their brothers' wrist*
Point to your Vishuddhi.	- *Neck*
What are the qualities of the Vishuddhi chakra?	- *Collectivity, diplomacy*
What countries represents the Vishuddhi?	- *North, Central and South America Scandinavian countries, some Eastern European countries*
What should you do when you feel no vibrations?	- *Work on the Vishuddhi chakra*
How many petals does the Vishuddhi chakra have?	- *Sixteen (16)*
On your hands, show which fingers are your Vishuddhi.	- *Both index fingers*

HAMSA CHAKRA

Deity:	Hamsa Chakra Swamini
Right Hamsa quality:	Common sense
Left Hamsa quality:	Intuition
Chakra controls:	Nose, sinuses
Oil:	Ghee, olive oil
Position:	Between the eyebrows
Animal:	Swan
Country:	Canada, New York
Causes of obstruction:	Extreme behaviour, dry conditions, spicy or sour food
Clearing:	Ghee or butter in the nose, use humidifiers, neti pot clearing

Ganas are soldiers of Shri Shiva's army.

"Hamsa chakra is located below the Agnya, where both the Ida and Pingala nadi come together and cross over. Two eyes represent the left and the right side. So this center is very much guided by our eyes, by our ears, by our nose, tongue, teeth and throat."
— Shri Mataji Nirmala Devi

The Hamsa chakra stands between the Vishuddhi and the Agnya.

"Discretion is the main quality of this chakra. Discretion is very beautifully described in the life of Shri Krishna. We can call Him that He had a naughty way of using His discretion. So on one side we have the help of Shri Krishna to give us the discretion, and on the other side we have Christ.

The discretion of the right side is Ham, and the discretion of the left side is Sa. Sa means `you', means `you are the one'. Hamsa, is made of two types of discretion, where to see `I am', and where to see `you are'. On these two balances, as they are shown here beautifully, the moon and the sun, in the center is the cross, which gives you the balance, which gives you the dharma, pure intelligence in a Hamsa."
— Shri Mataji Nirmala Devi

The hamsa chakra lies outside the path of the Kundalini.

"This chakra helps you to soothe down. Put ghee in hot water or milk and take it so that you soothe down your nerves and you smooth down your Vishuddhi. Put oil in your ears, into your nose not the oil but ghee. Brush your teeth at least twice daily. Put kajal in eyes and massage your hair with oil."

- Shri Mataji Nirmala Devi

Saturn, with another moon that rotates around it: This moon is called Titan and represents the Hamsa chakra.

What is the difference between a swan and a crane?

"Both the swan as well as the crane are white birds. What is the difference between the swan and a crane? The answer is that when you mix milk with water, the swan will just suck in the milk, leaving the water behind. The crane on the other hand has no discretion, it will drink the mixed liquid. Once we start loosing our discretionary power, people start becoming just like robots, because there is no personality. Anybody can brainwash us. That explains why people, so many thousands of people, take to wrong thinking. Their discretion is lacking."

- Shri Mataji Nirmala Devi

left top - crane   right - swan

The Sanskrit word for swan is hamsa. In India, swans are compared to saintly persons, whose characteristic is to be in the world without getting attached to it, just as a swan's feathers do not not get wet, although they are in water.

"We have never yet paid much attention to this center of Hamsa, which is, I think, very important for the Western world. The reason is, at the Hamsa Chakra part of the left side and right side come out and show themselves. So this Hamsa Chakra is the one, as it has not gone up to the Agnya, but is holding on certain threads or certain parts of the left and right side, and they start flowing toward your nose, expressing through your eyes, from your mouth and from your forehead.

The best way to balance the nadis at Hamsa is by breathing exercise.

Breathe in through one nostrill, hold the breath for a while, then let it out through the other nostrill. Do this three times, and very slowly.

Vishuddhi is an important chakra because it has a very great manifestation also. For example it has another, you can say a subsidiary chakra, which we call as Hamsa chakra. And the star, which is increasing this center, we say, the star that resides on which this center is working, is Saturn. And as you know with Saturn, there is another small little Saturn moving. In the same way with this Vishuddhi chakra, there's another one, which is a very important chakra, which we call as Hamsa chakra."

- *Shri Mataji Nirmala Devi*

The Hamsa chakra gives us discretion and common sense. This energy center give us understanding of what is good and what is bad behavior.

"When this center is alert and awakened, then we immediately know what is auspicious and what is not auspicious. Or we can call it – we get the divine discretion. I think, it is a part of the genetics that people have discretion between good and bad, destructive and constructive."

- *Shri Mataji Nirmala Devi*

Questions and Answers:

Does the Kundalini go through the Hamsa?	- *No, the Hamsa lies outside the path of the Kundalini*
What are Ganas?	- *The soldiers of Shri Shiva's army*
What country represents the Hamsa chakra?	- *Canada*
What animal represents the Hamsa chakra?	- *A swan*
Where can you find the Hamsa chakra?	- *Between the eyebrows*
What is intuition?	- *Intuition means that we take the help of the ganas, which surround us*

AGNYA CHAKRA

Deities:	Lord Jesus Christ, Mother Mary
	L - Shri Mahavira
	R - Shri Buddha
Number of petals:	2
Body part:	Brain; the Agnya chakra controls our sight, thoughts and all mental activity
Musical instrument:	Sarod
Color:	White
Element:	Light
Countries:	Jerusalem, Bethlehem, Palestine, Russia - ego
	China - superego
Oil:	Eucalyptus
Location on the hands:	Ring fingers
Precious stone:	Diamond
Symbol:	The cross
Astral connection:	The sun
Qualities:	Forgiveness, compassion, innocence
Causes of obstruction:	Roving eyes, bad company, too much reading or watching TV, unforgiving nature, worries
Clearing:	Look at the bindi of Shri Mataji's photo through a candle flame, put a bindi on your forehead for sleeping

A difficult chakra to keep open in human beings is the Agnya chakra because it is where our brain is and where all our thinking happens. Until the mind slows down and our thoughts cease, the Agnya chakra will not be fully clear. The Agnya chakra is the space between the ego and super-ego. When the balloons of the ego and super-ego deflate, the Kundalini can pass through the Agnya chakra.

Lord Jesus Christ in Art

Michelangelo was a realized soul, a great artist, who painted the Last Judgement of Christ on the dome of the Sistine Chapel in Italy. Michelangelo realized that Lord Jesus Christ was a strong and healthy young person, full of strength and in good health, unlike many other artists who showed Christ as weak and suffering.

> Lord Jesus was born without the earth element in His body, thus He consisted entirely of vibrations.

The Sistine Chapel in the Vatican was painted by Michelangelo. It took him 4 years to complete his master piece.

Lord Jesus Christ was born to open the Agnya chakra for mankind. He was born in a humble manger in Bethlehem, full of cattle. On the night Lord Jesus Christ was born, He was visited by 3 kings of the Orient, who were none other than Shri Brahma, Shri Vishnu, and Shri Shiva. The 3 kings did not know, where the young king was born, so to find Him, They followed a bright star, a comet, that guided Their way. When the three kings reached Bethlehem, They bowed with great humility before the little child and offered Their gifts: gold, frankincense, and myrrh.

From the time Lord Jesus Christ was born, He was extremely obedient, kind, and protective of His Mother. Mother Mary was the incarnation of Shri Mahalakshmi, and Lord Jesus Christ always wanted others to show Her respect.

"**Easter** is celebrated to show that Christ resurrected Himself. The Resurrection of Christ took place to open our Agnya chakra, because it is a very tight, subtle center. The conditionings and ego make it difficult for the Kundalini to go beyond the Agnya. Christ's own sacrifice on the cross and His resurrection had created a way for all of us to get into a new, transformed state. A state of the spirit."

- *Shri Mataji Nirmala Devi*

Lord Jesus Christ is also in control of Ekadesha Rudra and it's 11 destructive powers.

What's the meaning of offering eggs on Easter?

"An egg is offered because it can go into a transformation. First the bird is born as an egg and then reborn as a bird. When you get this egg as a symbol of Easter it means you can become a different person, someone who knows the spirit. So a human being is born as an individual separated from the spirit, and then is born the second time as a realized soul."   - *Shri Mataji Nirmala Devi*

"The larger the power of forgiveness the more powerful you will be. Forgive everyone. Only the one who is big can forgive. You are standing in dharma. The one who is standing in dharma has such tremendous powers within. Dharma is nothing but love. And if love is everything then forgiveness becomes its part. Everything will be washed away with love. Forgiveness is one of the qualities of the spirit."

— *Shri Mataji Nirmala Devi*

The bija mantra for the Agnya chakra is Ham - Ksham. We should say this mantra, when the ego and superego trouble us.

How to steady the Agnya?

People have wobbling eyes, wobbling Agnya and they need to steady their eyes, they have to soothe them. The most soothing thing for the eyes is the green grass. Walk with your eyes on the ground, then the Agnya chakra will be alright.

— *Shri Mataji Nirmala Devi*

Questions and Answers:

Where is the Agnya chakra located?	- In the center of the forehead
Why do we celebrate Easter?	- Lord Jesus Christ resurrected from death
Who is the incarnation of Shri Ganesha?	- Lord Jesus Christ
Who were the 3 kings who came to meet Lord Jesus Christ when he was born?	- Shri Brahma, Shri Shiva and Shri Vishnu
Why was Lord Jesus Christ born?	- To free us of our ego and super-ego
What is the greatest power of Lord Jesus Christ?	- The power of forgiveness
In Sahaja Yoga, what does the second birth mean?	- Self-realization
Why do we give an egg on Easter day?	- It signifies a second birth, a transformation
What is the name of Lord Jesus Christ's mother?	- Mother Mary
What brought the three kings to Bethlehem?	- A comet

Christ absorbed the sins of people through His compassion and forgiveness.

AGNYA CHAKRA - RIGHT

Deity:	Lord Buddha
Chakra controls:	Sight, thought
Country:	Russia
Palm location:	Ring fingers
Qualities:	Ego, "I-ness"
Causes of obstruction:	Vanity, egoism, criticism
Clearing:	"Shri Mataji, by Your grace, please, keep me in Your divine attention". "Shri Mataji, I forgive everyone, including myself". Forgive everyone. Do not hold grudges, to forgive is the most simple thing to do.

Buddha works on our right side, on our Agnya.

Siddhartha Gautama (Lord Buddha's name before he had received his self-realization) was born as a wealthy prince in India.

During a name choosing ceremony, a group of astrologers predicted that the young prince would grow up to be either a great emperor or become a sage (wise man). The prince grew up within the palace walls, shielded from the ugliness of the world beyond.

Growing up: one day, Prince Siddhartha finally persuaded His father to let Him go outside the palace walls to see the city. Gautama's father had ordered the city streets cleared of anyone who was old or sick. However, on His journey, Gautama came across a feeble old man who was lying at the side of the road. Struck by what was different from anything He had ever seen before, Siddhartha asked someone to explain, what was wrong with the man. Siddhartha was very moved by the suffering of the old man. He journeyed out into the city three more times and saw a sick man, a dead man and a sage.

Lord Buddha, as you know, is working on our right side and on our Agnya. He said, for the right side, you should be detached, desireless.

Determined to learn about what makes people sad, Siddhartha left His life of comfort at the palace and set out to seek answers to His questions. Siddhartha wandered through

the forests, discussing His questions with saints and sages. However, this did not bring Him satisfaction or greater understanding. Finally, Siddhartha settled under a tree to meditate. After many days of meditating, Siddhartha achieved enlightenment. From that point, He was known as the Buddha. For the rest of His life, the Buddha travelled around sharing His teachings with many people.

Banyan tree

In the Gujarati language, Banyan means grocer/merchant. In 1634, English writers began to tell of the Banyan tree, a tree under which Hindu merchants would conduct their business. The tree provided a shaded place for village meetings or for merchants to sell their goods. Eventually "Banyan" became the name of the tree itself.

"Buddha came to this earth at a time when it was so important for Him to come. In His time there were two types of people: those who were very **ritualistic**, trying to be extremely strict and disciplined; and the others were the people, who were **conditioned** and were full of so-called devotion to God. So these two types of people were occupying the area of seekers. It was necessary to overcome these two styles of seeking.

Buddha knew that the greatest problem of human beings is their ego. He said that "If you become desireless, then there will be no problem for you".

So to be desireless is the best way to achieve self-realization. But how to become desireless? You are sitting in the sand, and if you see, the sand doesn't get attached to anything. You put anything on it, it will not spoil anything. You put water, it will stick on, and as soon as you try to throw it away the whole thing will disappear into thin air. So to develop that kind of detachment, or to develop a life which was desireless was His aim. And that's why I say He was a disciple principle."

- Shri Mataji Nirmala Devi

Buddha wanted people first to get their realization.

Buddha taught people three important principles:

1) Surrender yourself to your spirit.

2) Surrender yourself to the religion, which is Vishwa Nirmala Dharma

3) Surrender yourselves to dharma.

Buddha and the Bandit

Buddha was once threatened with death by a bandit called Angulimal.

"Then be good enough to fulfill my dying wish," said Buddha. "Cut off the branch of that tree."

One slash of the sword, and it was done!

"What now?" asked the bandit.

"Put it back again," said Buddha.

The bandit laughed. "You must be crazy to think that anyone can do that."

"On the contrary, it is you who are crazy to think that you are mighty because you can wound and destroy. That is the task of children. The mighty know how to create and heal."

The moral of this story is that it is easy to take to destruction, but it takes a great person to heal or create something beautiful.

> Buddha, when He was born, He found that there was misery everywhere. And the misery, according to Him, was due to the desires we have. So to be desireless is the best way to achieve self-realization.

Questions and Answers:

What was Buddha's name when He was young?	- Siddhartha Gautama
What was Shri Buddhas message to us?	- To be without desire
What is ritualism?	- The practice of religious rituals
Why was Buddha born?	- To help human beings overcome the ego
What does the name Buddha mean?	- The enlightened one
What is the moral of the "Buddha and the Bandit" story?	- It is easy to destroy, but to create and heal it takes a great person.
Sitting under what tree did Lord Buddha get his self-realization?	- Under a Banyan tree

> Buddha realized the greatest problem of human beings is their ego.

Banyan tree fruits (figs).

SAHASRARA CHAKRA

MONDAY

Deity:	Shri Kalki
Chakra controls:	Vibrations, cool breeze
Number of petals:	1000
Flower:	Lotus
Musical instrument:	Sitar
Color:	All the colors
Element:	All the elements
Country/geographic location:	Himalayas
Vehicle:	Horse
Location on hands:	Center of palms
Precious stone:	Pearl
Symbol:	Bandhan
Astral connection:	Pluto
Qualities:	Self-realization, silence, thoughtless awareness, absolute freedom, Joy and bliss
Cause of obstruction:	Doubt in God

Shri Mataji Nirmala Devi is the deity of the Sahasrara chakra. In Her incarnation as the Adi Shakti She integrates all the divine qualities and also acts as a catalyst. She was born on the 21st of March, 1923, in Chindwara, India. Her husband's name was Sir C.P. Shrivastava, and they had two beautiful daughters, Kalpana and Sadhana. Shri Mataji opened the collective Sahasrara, sitting at the seashore in Nargol, India, because She could not bear to see the seekers of truth being lost any longer. She awakened the Kundalini on the collective level in India on the 5th of May, 1970. One year later, in 1971, Shri Mataji started giving self-realization to a handful of people, and Sahaja Yoga was born. Shri Mataji travelled all over the world to give people their spiritual awakening.

At the level of Sahasrara you know the truth.

How to keep the Sahasrara chakra open?

"It is simple" says Shri Mataji Nirmala Devi. "You must fully and completely surrender to Me. In case you find your Sahasrara still closed, in that case you have to ask for forgiveness. You must ask, 'If I have made any mistake, please, forgive me!' Then you will feel cool vibrations flowing."

Chindhwara, India birthplace of Shri Mataji Nirmala Devi

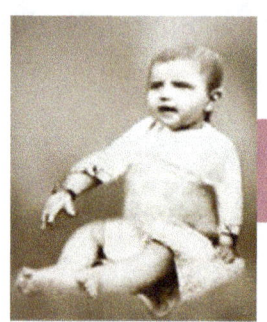
Young Nirmala

In 1970 Shri Mataji had declared that She was the Adi Shakti.

"... today, it is the day I declare: 'I am the one who has to save humanity. I declare I am the one who is Adi Shakti, who is the mother of all mothers, who is the primordial Mother. The Shakti of the desire of God, who has incarnated on this earth to give meaning to creation, to human beings. And I am sure that through My love and patience and My powers, I am going to achieve it."

- Shri Mataji Nirmala Devi

The past is finished whilst the future does not exist, so enjoy the present which is the reality.

What mountain range is this? (sayalamiH)

When the Kundalini reaches the Sahasrara chakra, the lotus petals of our Sahasrara open and self-realization takes place. We may feel a pulsation at the crown of the head, followed by a gentle cool breeze coming out of the top of our head.

The Sahasrara chakra is actually the assemblage of the six lower chakras. It is a hollow space, on the sides of which there are one thousand nadis (nerves). And when the Kundalini energy penetrates into the limbic area, then the enlightenment of these nadis takes place, and they can be perceived as flames, gentle, steady flames, in all the seven colors of the rainbow (VIBGYOR). The last flame, ultimately, when integrated, becomes a crystal clear flame. All the seven chakras become crystal clear when they integrate in the Sahasrara. When the Sahasrara is enlightened, it takes the form of a bundle of steadily burning flames.

"We have to show the results of Kundalini awakening. It's not only for you. It's for the whole world."
- Shri Mataji Nirmala

On May 5th, 1970, Shri Mataji opened the collective Sahasrara in Nargol, India.

"As soon as the Sahasrara was opened, the whole atmosphere was filled with tremendous chaitanya (vibrations), and there was tremendous light in the sky, and the whole thing came on this earth, as if a torrential rain or a waterfall with such tremendous force as if I was unaware and got amazed. The happening was so tremendous, and so unexpected that I was stunned and got totally silent at the grandeur. I saw the primordial Kundalini rising like a big furnace, and the furnace was very silent but a burning appearance it had, as if you heat up a metal, and it had many colors."

— Shri Mataji Nirmala Devi

The truth is that you are not this body, this mind, this ego, these conditionings, but you are the pure spirit. - Shri Mataji Nirmala Devi

Shri Mataji Nirmala Devi and Her husband Sir. C.P.

"You must have full faith in the paramchaitanya (the all pervading power). As soon as you get detached and ask the divine power to work things out for you, then nature takes over. But if you think that `you' are going to solve your problems, then the divine power says `Alright, try your luck'. When you are detached, then everything works out very well." — Shri Mataji Nirmala Devi

Questions and Answers:

How many petals does the Sahasrara chakra have?	- 1000 petals
When was Shri Mataji born?	- March 21st, 1923
When did Shri Mataji open the Sahasrara chakra?	- May 5th, 1970
Shri Mataji is the incarnation of which deity?	- Shri Adishakti
What flower is part of Shri Mataji's name?	- Daisy
Where did Shri Mataji open the Sahasrara chakra?	- At Nargol, India
What precious stone represents the Sahasrara?	- The pearl
What is the flower of the Sahasrara?	- The lotus
Where was Shri Mataji born?	- In Chindwara, India
What is the colors of the Sahasrara chakra?	- The Sahasrara has all the color of the rainbow

IDA NADI (LEFT SIDE)

Deity:	Shri Mahakali, Shri Bhairava
Nadi controls:	Emotions, our past, existence
Color:	light blue, becomes black when exhausted
Represents:	Past
Color:	Light blue
Location on the hands:	Left hand
Symbol:	Moon
River:	The Ganges river
Qualities:	Good health, emotional balance
Causes of obstruction:	Lethargy, depression
Clearing:	Use all techniques to warm up the left side. Use candle treatment. Eat protein rich food.

The Ganges valley stretches wide across Northern India and Bangladesh, from the Himalayas to the Bay of Bengal.

"Shri Mahakali is the one who relaxes you completely. When you are tired, She makes you sleep like a baby. In Her lap you sleep nicely, quietly and all your problems get solved. She appears to you in deep sleep, when you dream, She brings forth solutions to your problems, She guides you and tells you what to do. Many people have told Me: "Mother, You came in my dream and told me that this is the medicine I should take to recover." or "Mother, You came in my dream and You said that You are in Bombay". In your dreams, you see Me clearly and that happening is thanks to Shri Mahakali. Shri Mahakali destroys all the enemies that stand in your way, all the rakshasas and all the negative forces, so that your are all right."

— Shri Mataji Nirmala Devi

The Shri Mahakali power creates illusion. She puts you in maya. She wants to test you.

"Shri Mahakali has a double role all the time, She is at two extremes. On one side She is full of joy, giver of joy, She is very happy when She sees Her disciples are joyous. Joy is Her own quality, is Her energy. The other side of Her is the one who is extremely cruel, wrathful. She is the one who is the slayer of those people who try to do evil."

— Shri Mataji Nirmala Devi

"Shri Mahakali destroys all that troubles us, gives us comfort of the spirit so that we can live happily anywhere. She comforts our bodies so that diseases are destroyed, and we feel yournger and more energetic. She is the giver of good memory and above all She also gives us the highest boon (blessing), the boon of JOY.

When we have a strong Mooladhara, then the Mahakali power is the strongest within us. To get into the center, to achieve balance, first we move out of the left side to the right side, and from there to the center. If you are feeling lethargic, unable to get up, or are feeling sleepy, plan what you will do next and spring into action. Even doing a puja is a good idea, it awakens bhakti (devotion) within us."

- Shri Mataji Nirmala Devi

Shri Bhairava is the greatest disciple of Shri Mahakali. He lived 12,000 years ago and was reborn as William Blake in England (1757 - 1827). Shri Bhairava cools us down by destroying all negativities in our left side. He is also the archangel Michael.

Left side treatments:

- Use the lemon treatment by holding a vibrated lemon in the left hand while meditating.
- To clear the left side, sit in the sunlight and use candle treatment.
- Use a matka treatment (seven chillies and seven lemons)
- To clear your back Agnya, sit with your back Agnya toward the morning sun.
- Move a candle and run it up and down along the left channel.

Ganges river

To cure left sided problems, you have to take to the fire or to the sun or to the flames.

"Bhairava runs up and down the Ida nadi. The Ida nadi is the nadi of Chandrama, is of the moon. So this is a channel for us to cool down. So the work of Bhairavaji is to cool us down. People have a hot temper with their ego, with their liver, whatever it is, and if a person is in a big temper, then Bhairava plays tricks on that person to cool him down. He organizes everything under His own control with the gana's help, with Ganapati's help, to cool down your temperament, to give you a balance."

- Shri Mataji Nirmala Devi

Shri Mahakali exposes all that is wrong, all that is falsehood, that is untruth.

"When you have fire, we call it as Agni, it is a very silent fire, it does not burn anybody, but it burns all the wrong things within you, and it burns all the wrong things within other people as well. When you become a good Sahaja Yogi - and I should say a perfect Sahaja Yogi - fire will never burn you. We have an example of Sitaji and how She went into the fire...nothing happened to Her...
Fire is the purifier and should be used to clear the left side. Just ask the fire to take away your problems. Fire burns, gives light, it cooks, and nourishes. If the flame in front of My photo starts flickering, that is alright and that means there is a problem and it is being corrected by My photo. Baddhas can be burned off by the fire, by the flame and are to be seen as flickering of the flame. Sometimes, the flame can also go pop, pop sound."

— Shri Mataji Nirmala Devi

Shri Mahakali destroys all negative forces within us. The six negative forces to our spiritual growth are: **lust, anger, greed, attachment, jealousy** and **vanity**. Once Shri Mahakali destroys these six enemies within us, then only we become the spirit.

Shri Mahakali controls our emotions.

Questions and Answers:

How can we clear negativity of the left side? — By using the fire element

What river represents the left side? — The river Ganges

Who was the second incarnation of Shri Bhairava? — William Blake

What is the color of a healthy left side? — Light blue

What are the six enemies within us? — Lust (Mooladhara), anger (Swadhistana), greed (Nabhi) attachment (Anahata), jealousy (Vishuddhi), and vanity (Agnya)

PINGALA NADI (RIGHT SIDE)

Deities:	Shri Hanuman, Shri Mahasaraswati
Nadi controls:	Physical and mental activities
Country:	Germany
Represents:	Future
Color:	Orange, becomes dark red when exhausted
Location on the hands:	Entire right hand
Planet/astral body:	Sun
River:	Yamuna
Qualities:	Dynamism, pure devotion
Clearing:	Use a cold water foot soak, Put an ice pack on the liver

The sun is a star. A star does not have a solid surface, but is a ball of gas that is held together by its own gravity.

Shri Hanumana controls and protects the right side of our subtle (energy) system. He is a great and powerful warrior, dynamic, playful and childlike. He is fully devoted to Shri Rama and Shri Sita. He is Their messenger and loves nothing more than singing songs in Their praise. He is the king of monkeys, and the son of the wind-god Vayu. He is as strong as a lion and moves as fast as the wind. Thus moving swiftly from the Swadisthana up to the brain Shri Hanuman supplies the brain with all it needs to function well, for example He transforms sugar into fat cells (gray matter).

Shri Hanuman creates all electromagnetic forces.

Shri Lakshmana, Shri Rama's brother, got hit by a poison arrow from evil Ravana. Lord Rama was very distressed at seeing His brother about to die. Physicians were called, and one said he could cure Shri Lakshmana with the herb Sanjivani. The herb could be found on top of Mount Meru in the Himalayas. Upon hearing this Shri Hanumana left without hesitation to fetch the herb. He flew all the way to the Himalayas and found the mountain, but when He arrived, He could not tell which one was the Sanjivani herb. Again, Shri Hanumana did not hesitate. He grew to an enormous size and took the entire peak in His hands and carried it back to

His lord. This way the physician himself could pick the right plant. This is how Shri Hanumana helped save Shri Lakshmana's life, and His lord Rama was very pleased with Him for His quick thinking.

Young Hanuman eats the sun.

As a child, believing the sun to be a ripe mango, Hanuman pursued it in order to eat it. Rahu was seeking out the sun at that same time, and he clashed with Hanuman. Hanuman was stronger than Rahu and continued to try to take the sun in His mouth. Rahu approached Indra, king of the devas, and complained that a monkey child stopped him from reaching the sun, thereby preventing the scheduled eclipse. This enraged Indra, who responded by throwing the Vajra (thunderbolt) at Hanuman, which struck His jaw. Hanuman fell back down to the earth and became unconscious. The devas later on revived Hanuman and blessed Him with multiple boons.

Shri Brahma also said, "Nobody will be able to kill You with any weapons in war." From Shri Brahma He obtained the power of inducing fear in enemies, and destroying fear in friends, to be able to change His form at will and to be able to easily travel wherever He wishes to go. From Shri Shiva He obtained the ability to cross the ocean. Shri Shiva assured the safety of Shri Hanuman with an arm band that would protect Him for life. Indra blessed Him with complete protection from the Vajra weapon, thus it would no longer be effective on Him. Varuna, the lord of the sea, blessed young Hanuman with a boon that would always protect Him from the dangers of water. Agni blessed Him with immunity to the dangers of fire. Surya blessed Him with the ability to assume the smallest or the biggest form, as needed. Yama, the god of death blessed him with a healthy life.

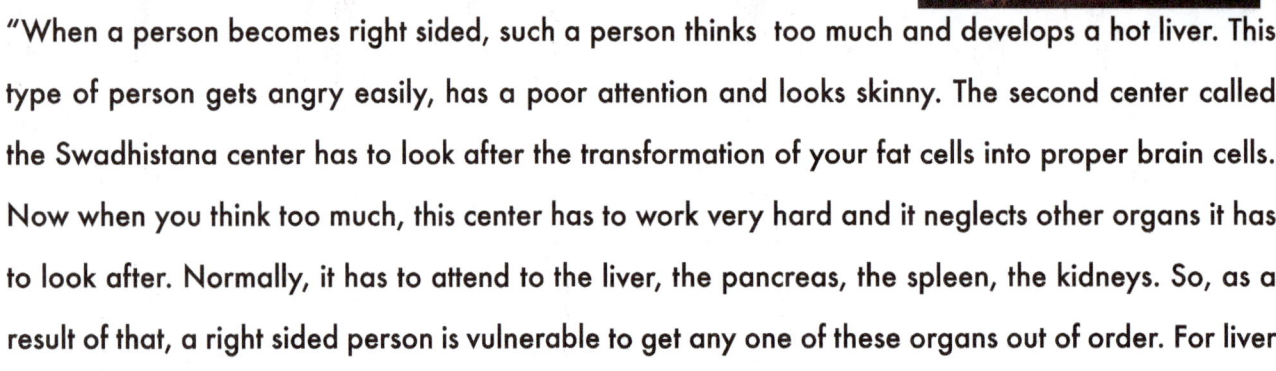

Image of the sun taken by the Hubble telescope.

The five elements are: water, earth, fire, air and ether.

"When a person becomes right sided, such a person thinks too much and develops a hot liver. This type of person gets angry easily, has a poor attention and looks skinny. The second center called the Swadhistana center has to look after the transformation of your fat cells into proper brain cells. Now when you think too much, this center has to work very hard and it neglects other organs it has to look after. Normally, it has to attend to the liver, the pancreas, the spleen, the kidneys. So, as a result of that, a right sided person is vulnerable to get any one of these organs out of order. For liver problems, drink several glasses of water per day. This works to flush away toxins."

- *Shri Mataji Nirmala Devi*

The right side sympathetic nervous system is the power of action, that acts through the five elements (fire, earth, air, water, ether). The Pingala nadi (right channel) is golden, orange and then red. When the right side heats up, a person becomes aggressive and futuristic. This channel contains heat and needs cooling down. It is the side of our mental activity, the future, planning and of the ego. Fumes from the activity on the right side collect in the balloon of the ego and cause the Sahasrara to close. To get into balance from the right side, we do not do so by going into the left side, but by getting into the center by developing the witness state. You must say, "I am not doing it."

- Shri Mataji Nirmal Devi

He is the one who is always anxious to do the work of Shri Rama.

To cool down your right side (liver), follow these steps:

- Drink kokum juice
- Go on a liver diet
- Do a cool water foot soak
- Drink vibrated water with sugar
- Meditate with the left hand toward the sky
- Put attention on nature
- When meditating, sit on the mother earth
- Surrender yourself to Shri Mataji
- Body massage with coconut or almond oil
- Put ice on your liver and right hand toward Shri Mataji

Shri Hanuman is the archangel Gabriel, the divine messenger, the one who told Mary that She was to give birth to Jesus Christ.

Questions and Answers:

Name all the five elements.	- Water, earth, air, fire, ether
Name 2 ways of cooling down your liver.	- Go on a liver diet, put ice on the liver
Which channel does Shri Hanumana control?	- The right side (Pingala nadi)
Shri Hanuman is an angel called …?	- Archangel Gabriel
Who is the doer of miracles in Sahaja Yoga?	- Shri Hanuman
What country represents the right side?	- Germany
Who is the deity of the right side?	- Shri Hanuman
What is electromagnetic force?	- It is a special force that affects everything in the universe

SUSHUMNA NADI (CENTRAL CHANNEL)

Deity:	Shri Mahalakshmi
Nadi controls:	Autonomous nervous system (whose functions include breathing and the heart beat)
Color:	Gold
Represents:	Present
Location on hands:	Both hands (left and right)
River:	River Saraswati
Qualities:	Balance, silence
Clearing:	Balance your left and right side

Our seeking starts from the Mahalakshmi principle.

Shri Mahalakshmi presides over our central channel, called the Sushumna nadi. This nadi regulates our autonomous nervous system, which means, it looks after some of our bodily functions without our control, such as ensuring the beating of our heart, our digestion, breathing, and much more. The Sushumna nadi is the central channel of our subtle system. The Mother Kundalini rises from the sacrum (=holy) bone area to the Sahasrara chakra through this nadi. When we offer a puja, this channel opens wide and makes it easy for the Mother Kundalini to reach our Sahasrara and flow through the fontanel bone area like a little fountain (fontanel means little fountain).

Shri Mahalakshmi has incarnated five times: Shri Sita, Shri Radha, Mother Mary, Shri Fatima, Shri Adi Shakti Mataji.

Shri Mahalakshmi is one of the aspects of Shri Adi Shakti along with Shri Mahakali and Shri Mahasaraswati. Shri Mahalakshmi was born out of the ocean when Sur and Asur were churning the ocean for amrut. Standing on a lotus Shri Mahalakshmi shows balance and knows how to handle people delicately. She does not like it when people do wrong things, and She does not give Her blessings to such people.

She holds a lotus in Her hand. The beautiful lotus flower grows out of the mud, and a lotus welcomes all kinds of bugs like worthy guests. Shri Mahalakshmi tells us to model our hearts after the lotus flower and receive others with unconditional love. Shri Mahalakshmi's power purifies us and others, thus wherever we Sahaja yogis go, we purify places and people too.

The Mahalakshmi principle lies within all of us in the center, and once you are tired with the falsehood and also with the hypocrisy of people, you start seeking the truth within. That is how a new category of people is born. They are called seekers. They are very different from others. They do not care for being successful, money hungry or doing wrong things. They want to seek the truth. Sahaja yogis fall in this category and that is why you came to Sahaja Yoga.

What river am I? (itawsaraS revir)

Keep your Sushumna open, then there will be no physical problems, no emotional problems, and of course no spiritual problems.
- Shri Mataji Nirmala Devi

"The central path of Sushumna is for people who are in the center, who are wise. They are generous, tactful and diplomatic. They keep calm, never show off, they keep quiet. I know who those people are. At the same time, they are dynamic, they work things out only when they have something important to do. They are beautiful, gracious people."
                                                                                                            - Shri Mataji Nirmala Devi

"The Sushumna nadi is the axis of the mother earth. There is an energy force within the mother earth. This energy force acts in such a manner that the earth moves with such tremendous speed. It not only moves but it creates day and night for us, so that in the day-time we can work, and during the night-time we can sleep, to give us balance. The earth moves in such a manner around the sun that half of the countries get a lot of sun during summer-time, and half of them get it during winter-time. That's the axis that acts and works out everything. Apart from that, this axis keeps all the necessary distances from the other planets and other moving bodies in the cosmos.

This axis is the intelligence and the fragrance of the mother earth. Now through this axis only all these swayambhus and all these great happenings of earthquakes take place. This axis is the one which moves the lava into different directions and pierces through different areas to create earth quakes, and also to have ... volcanoes. And all these things happen because the axis has a sense of what is to be done. This axis is one that loves us. Because of this axis we have seasons."
                                                                                                            - Shri Mataji Nirmala Devi

The Sushumna nadi is the axis of the Mother Earth.

"The seasons are created beautifully to give us different varieties of food and varieties of things. The heat of the mother earth, if it is lost, then we'll have nothing on this Earth, it'll be all frozen and there will be all snow, and we'll have no food, nothing, and it will be like on the moon living here."

- Shri Mataji Nirmala Devi

Our seasons change because of the tilt of the Earth on its axis as it orbits the sun. As the earth travels there are times when we are closer to the sun (summer) and times when we are further away from the sun (winter).

winter   spring   summer   autumn

How to balance yourself?

Bring your attention to the centre. To do this, first bring it to the right side by saying the Gayatri mantra. Then to the centre by saying the Shri Brahmadeva-Saraswati mantra. On moving to the right, you start feeling vibrations, stop at this point. Do not say any more Gayatri mantras because you must not go too much to the right. Too much to the right means the frequency of vibrations starts decreasing. It is important that you must get the vibrations. If not, then repeatedly raise the Kundalini until you feel the vibrations.

Another way is to put the left hand towards My photograph and the right hand on the ground. Say the Shri Mahakali mantra so that the vibrations start flowing. Using a candle from behind on the left side will also help.   - Shri Mataji Nirmala Devi

Questions and Answers:

"I am balanced."

What deity rules the central channel?	- Shri Mahalakhsmi
Along which channel does the Kundalini rise?	- The Sushumna nadi (center)
What hand represents the right side?	- The right hand
What river represents the Sushumna nadi?	- The river Saraswati
What are the four seasons?	- Spring, summer, autumn, winter
Name the five incarnations of Shri Mahalakshmi?	- Shri Sita, Shri Radha, Mother Mary, Shri Fatima, Shri Mataji

www.ingramcontent.com/pod-product-compliance
Lightning Source LLC
Chambersburg PA
CBHW060357010526
44109CB00051B/2503